Introduction

Quilters love precuts. It's hard to resist those curated bundles of joy that fabric stores have displayed all over! Fabric companies make it so easy by packaging whole collections into bundles of fat quarters, precut strips or 5" and 10" squares.

Of course, you will eventually want to create something with the fabrics you've collected! You'll find many creative ways to use your precuts within the pages of this pattern book.

Pull up a chair, grab your favorite beverage and start making a plan for your next project (or two!).

Table of Contents

DESIGN BY DEBI ESTLEMAN OF THREAD WEST
QUILTED BY KATIE LUYK OF THIRD COAST QUILTING

Needlepoint

Make this spin-off of the classic double link block that suggests both needles and cross stitch.

SKILL LEVEL
Confident Beginner

FINISHED SIZES
Quilt Size: 74½" x 88"
Block Size: 12½" x 12½"
Number of Blocks: 30

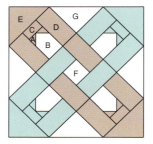

Needlepoint
12½" x 12½" Finished Block
Make 30

MATERIALS
- 30 assorted print fat quarters*
- 3¾ yards ivory solid*
- ¾ yard aqua print*
- 7¼ yards backing*
- 82" x 96" batting*
- Basic sewing tools and supplies

*Fabrics from the Bee Dots and Bee
Vintage Basics collections by Lori Holt
and the Confetti Cotton collection for
Riley Blake Designs; Heirloom Premium
80/20 batting from Hobbs Bonded
Fibers used to make sample. EQ8 was
used to design this quilt.*

PROJECT NOTES
Read all instructions before beginning
this project.
Stitch right sides together using a
¼" seam allowance unless otherwise
specified.

Materials and cutting lists assume 40"
of usable fabric width for yardage and
20" for fat quarters.
Arrows indicate directions to press
seams.
WOF – width of fabric
HST – half-square triangle
QST – quarter-square triangle

CUTTING

From each print fat quarter cut:
- 2 (4⅝") E squares, then cut once
  diagonally
- 12 (2¼" x 4") D rectangles
- 4 (1⅜" x 2¼") C rectangles
- 8 (1⅜") A squares

From ivory solid cut:
- 30 (6¼") G squares, then cut twice
  diagonally
- 120 (2¼" x 3⅛") B rectangles
- 30 (2¼") F squares
- 24 (1½" x 13") H strips
- 8 (4½" x WOF) strips, stitch short ends
  to short ends, then subcut into:
      2 (4½" x 80½") J and 2 (4½" x 75")
      K border strips
- 9 (1½" x WOF) strips, stitch short ends
  to short ends, then subcut into:
      5 (1½" x 67") I sashing strips

From aqua print cut:
- 9 (2½" x WOF) binding strips

Here Are Tips

Layer fat quarters to cut multiple pieces at once. Install a new rotary blade for this time-saving method, both for safety and precision, and start with fewer layers to determine how many you can cut and still maintain accuracy.

Use leftover print fabrics instead of the aqua print for the binding if desired. Cut 23 (2½" x 18") strips, sew together end to end using diagonal seams and bind with your favorite method.

COMPLETING THE BLOCKS

1. Each block requires two sets of contrasting print pieces, each set including four A squares, two C rectangles, six D rectangles and two E triangles. You will also need four B rectangles, one F square and four G triangles of the ivory solid. Select all the pieces for your first block.

2. Refer to Sew & Flip Corners on page 5 and add two A squares of your first print to a B rectangle as shown (Figure 1). Make two A-B-A units using the first print and two using the second print.

A-B-A Unit
Make 2 sets of 2
matching per block

Figure 1

3. Sew a matching C rectangle to an A-B-A unit and then add matching D rectangles to the sides (Figure 2a). Sew a matching E triangle to the top, centering, to make a needlepoint unit (Figure 2b). Make two needlepoint units with the first print and two with the second print.

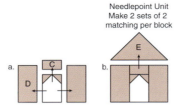

Needlepoint Unit
Make 2 sets of 2
matching per block

Figure 2

4. Refer to Partial Seams on page 5 and add two D rectangles of the first print and two of the second print to an F square in the arrangement shown to make a center unit (Figure 3).

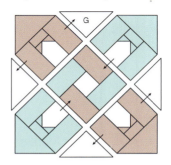

Center Unit
Make 1 per block

Figure 3

5. Arrange and sew three diagonal rows using four G triangles, two each of the needlepoint units and the center unit (Figure 4). Join the rows to complete a Needlepoint block.

Figure 4

6. Repeat steps 1–5 to make 30 total blocks.

COMPLETING THE QUILT

1. Referring to the Assembly Diagram, lay out the blocks in six rows of five blocks each. Add H strips between the blocks.

2. Sew the blocks and H strips into rows. Join the rows and the I sashing strips to complete the quilt center. Press.

3. Sew the J and K border strips to the quilt top in alphabetical order.

4. Layer, baste, quilt as desired and bind referring to Quilting Basics. The photographed quilt was quilted with an edge-to-edge point and loop design. ●

Needlepoint
Assembly Diagram 74½" x 88"

SEW & FLIP CORNERS

Use this method to add triangle corners in a quilt block.

1. Draw a diagonal line from corner to corner on the wrong side of the specified square. Place the square, right sides together, on the indicated corner of the larger piece, making sure the line is oriented in the correct direction indicated by the pattern (Figure 1).

2. Sew on the drawn line. Trim ¼" away from sewn line (Figure 2).

3. Open and press to reveal the corner triangle (Figure 3).

Figure 1

Figure 2

Figure 3

4. If desired, square up the finished unit to the required unfinished size. ●

PARTIAL SEAMS

Use partial seaming to join a variety of unevenly placed pieces in a block or unevenly placed blocks or sections in a quilt.

1. Lay out the block pieces or quilt sections around the center piece or block as shown in Figure A.

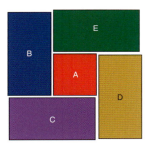

Figure A

2. Referring to Figure B, stitch A (center square) to B (first section) beginning approximately 2" from the bottom corner of A. Finger-press A away from B.

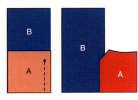

Figure B

3. Working counterclockwise, join C (second section) to the A-B unit as shown in Figure C, stitching the entire length of the seam. Press seam toward C.

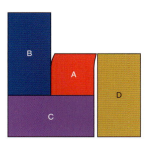

Figure C

4. Match and join D (third section) to A-C edge referring again to Figure C, completing the entire length of the seam. Press seam toward D.

5. Join E (fourth section) to the A-D edge, again completing the entire length of the seam, as shown in Figure D. Be sure to keep B (first section) out of the way when stitching.

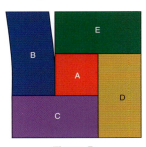

Figure D

6. Complete the assembly by finishing the A-B seam that was partially sewn in step 2. Fold over C and match the B edge to the A-E edge. Lower the machine needle at the end of the A-B seam, backstitch to secure and complete the A-B seam as shown in red in Figure E. Press seam toward B, completing the block or quilt section (Figure F). ●

Figure E

Figure F

Carnival Confetti

Quickly transform a bundle of 10 fat quarters into a fun, geometric throw quilt!

SKILL LEVEL
Confident Beginner

FINISHED SIZES
Quilt Size: 48" x 60"
Block Size: 12" x 12"
Number of Blocks: 20

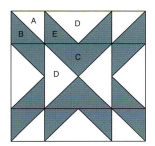

Carnival Confetti
12" x 12" Finished Block
Make 20

MATERIALS
- 10 assorted bright fat quarters*
- ⅝ yard teal batik*
- 2⅛ yards white tonal*
- 3¼ yards backing fabric*
- 56" x 68" batting*
- Thread
- Basic sewing tools and supplies

Fabrics from the 1895 Watercolors and 24/7 Solids collections from Hoffman Fabrics; Tuscany Wool/Cotton Blend batting from Hobbs Bonded Fibers used to make sample.

PROJECT NOTES
Read all instructions before beginning this project.

Stitch right sides together using a ¼" seam allowance unless otherwise specified.

Arrows indicate directions to press seams.

Materials and cutting lists assume 40" of usable fabric width for yardage and 20" for fat quarters.
WOF – width of fabric
HST – half-square triangle
QST – quarter-square triangle

CUTTING

From each fat quarter cut:
- 1 (7½") C square
- 8 (4¼") E squares
- 4 (4") B squares

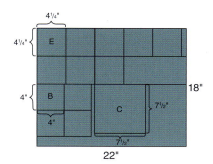

Fat Quarter
Cutting Diagram

From teal batik cut:
- 6 (2½" x WOF) binding strips

From white tonal cut:
- 30 (7½") D squares
- 40 (4") A squares

COMPLETING THE BLOCKS

1. Referring to Half-Square Triangles on page 9, make eight matching A-B units (Figure 1). Trim to measure 3½" square.

A-B Unit
Make 8

Figure 1

2. Again referring to Half-Square Triangles, use C and D squares to make two matching C-D units. Do not trim. Draw a diagonal line on the wrong side of one C-D unit, perpendicular to the seam line, and then pair the C-D units right sides together with colors opposite. Stitch ¼" on each side of the line, trim on the line, and press C-D units open (Figure 2). Square up to measure 6½". Make two.

C-D Unit
Make 2

Figure 2

3. Referring to Four-at-a-Time Flying Geese on page 9, use D and E squares to make eight matching D-E units (Figure 3).

D-E Unit
Make 8

Figure 3

4. Lay out one C-D unit, four A-B units and four D-E units into three rows of three units each (Figure 4). Sew the units into rows and join the rows to make one block. Make two.

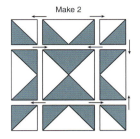

Make 2

Figure 4

5. Repeat steps 1–4 to make a total of 20 blocks.

COMPLETING THE QUILT

1. Lay out the blocks into five rows of four blocks. Sew blocks into rows and join the rows to complete the quilt center.

2. Layer, baste, quilt as desired and bind referring to Quilting Basics. The photographed quilt was quilted with a wavy stripe design. ●

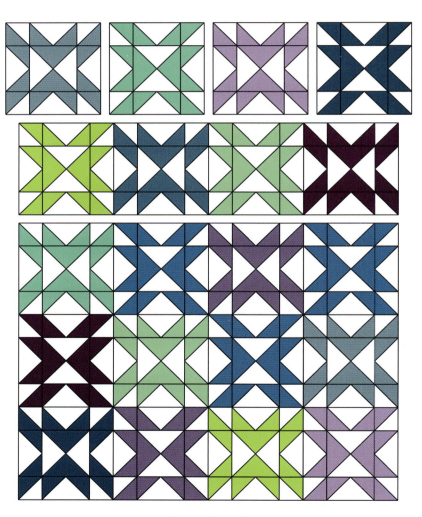

Carnival Confetti
Assembly Diagram 48" x 60"

HALF-SQUARE TRIANGLES

Half-square triangles (HSTs) are a basic unit of quilting used in many blocks or on their own. This construction method will yield two HSTs.

1. Refer to the pattern for size to cut squares. The standard formula is to add ⅞" to the finished size of the square. Cut two squares from different colors this size. For example, for a 3" finished HST unit, cut 3⅞" squares.

2. Draw a diagonal line from corner to corner on the wrong side of the lightest color square. Layer the squares right sides together. Stitch ¼" on either side of the drawn line (Figure A).

Figure A

3. Cut the squares apart on the drawn line, leaving a ¼" seam allowance and making two HST units referring to Figure B.

Figure B

4. Open the HST units and press seam allowances toward the darker fabric making two HST units (Figure C). ●

Figure C

FOUR-AT-A-TIME FLYING GEESE

With this method, smaller squares are sewn onto opposite ends of a larger square. The unit is cut in half and additional small squares are sewn on the units. After sewing in place and cutting, the small squares are flipped open to create the flying geese unit.

The large square will be the center of the flying geese units, and the small squares will become the "wings." The bias edges aren't exposed until after sewing, so there is no concern about stretch and distortion (Photo A).

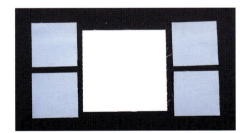

Photo A

Cutting
Refer to the pattern for the sizes to cut the rectangle and squares. Cut as directed in the pattern.

Determine the finished size of the flying geese unit you'd like to make and add 1¼" to the desired finished width of the flying geese unit, then cut one center square.

Add ⅞" to the height of the desired finished flying geese unit and cut four squares.

For example, to make four 2" x 4" finished flying geese units, cut one 5¼" square and four 2⅞" squares.

Assembly
1. Draw a diagonal line on the wrong side of each small square. Orienting the drawn lines as shown in photo, position two small squares on opposite corners of the large square. The small squares will overlap slightly in the middle. Stitch ¼" away from both sides of the marked line. Using a rotary cutter, cut on the marked line to create two units (Photo B).

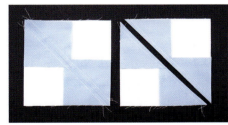

Photo B

2. Press seam allowances toward the small triangles.

3. Position the remaining squares on the units as shown and stitch ¼" away on each side of the marked line (Photo C).

Photo C

4. Cut on the marked line and press toward the triangles to create a total of four flying geese units (Photo D).

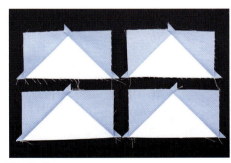

Photo D

5. If desired, trim dog-ears and square up the finished unit to the required unfinished size. ●

DESIGN BY WENDY SHEPPARD
QUILTED BY DARLENE SZABO OF SEW GRACEFUL QUILTING

Blooming Baskets

Pastel tonal fabrics make a fresh early spring palette.

SKILL LEVEL
Confident Beginner

FINISHED SIZES
Quilt Size: 73" x 73"
Block Size: 16" x 16" and 3" x 3"
Number of Blocks: 9 and 40

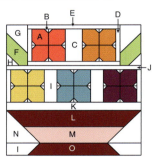

Basket
16" x 16" Finished Block
Make 9

Pinwheel
3" x 3" Finished Block
Make 40

PROJECT NOTES
Read all instructions before beginning this project.

Stitch right sides together using a ¼" seam allowance unless otherwise specified.

Materials and cutting lists assume 40" of usable fabric width for yardage and 20" for fat quarters.

Arrows indicate directions to press seams.

WOF – width of fabric
HST – half-square triangle
QST – quarter-square triangle

MATERIALS
- 1 fat quarter each red, orange, blue, plum, 2 yellows, dark red, aqua and green tonals*
- 1 fat quarter each light pink, light aqua, light yellow, light green and light purple tonals*
- 5 yards white tonal*
- 1 yard light blue tonal*
- 4½ yards backing*
- 81" x 81" batting*
- Thread*
- Basic sewing tools and supplies

Fabrics from Kimberbell Basics by Maywood Studio; 50 wt. thread from Aurifil; Tuscany Silk batting from Hobbs Bonded Fibers used to make sample. EQ8 was used to design this quilt.

CUTTING

From each red, orange, blue, plum and yellow 1 tonal cut:
- 36 (2½") A squares (180 total)

From each yellow 2, dark red and aqua tonal cut:
- 3 (2½" x 16½") L rectangles (9 total)
- 3 (2" x 11½") O rectangles (9 total)

From green tonal cut:
- 18 (3" x 4½") F rectangles

From each light pink, light aqua and light yellow tonal cut:
- 3 (2½" x 16½") M rectangles (9 total)
- 16 (2½") U squares (48 total)

From each light green and light purple tonal cut:
- 16 (2½") U squares (32 total)

"I wanted a quilt that reflects spring flowers brightening up the gardens after a long winter." —Wendy Sheppard

From length of white tonal cut:

- 2 (3½" x 54½") Q strips
- 2 (3" x 68½") X border strips
- 2 (3" x 63½") W border strips
- 2 (2" x 57½") S border strips
- 2 (2" x 54½") R border strips
- 18 (4½") N squares
- 6 (3½" x 16½") P rectangles
- 40 (3½") V squares
- 9 (2½" x 4½") C rectangles
- 18 (3" x 4") G rectangles
- 80 (2½") T squares
- 36 (2" x 4½") I rectangles
- 18 (2") H squares
- 9 (1½" x 16½") K rectangles
- 9 (1" x 16½") J rectangles
- 18 (1" x 11½") E rectangles
- 36 (1" x 4½") D rectangles
- 360 (1") B squares

From light blue tonal cut:

- 8 (3" x WOF) strips, stitch short ends to short ends, then subcut into:
  2 (3" x 73½") Z and 2 (3" x 68½") Y border strips

From remainder of fat quarters cut:

- 18 total (2½" x 20") binding strips

COMPLETING THE BLOCKS

Basket

1. Refer to Sew & Flip Corners on page 5 to add corner triangles on two diagonally opposite corners of one A square using two B squares to complete one A-B unit (Figure 1). Make 180.

A-B Unit
Make 180

Figure 1

2. Noting fabric orientation, arrange four matching A-B units in two rows; sew into rows, then sew the rows together to complete one flower unit (Figure 2). Make 45.

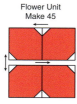

Flower Unit
Make 45

Figure 2

3. Position a G rectangle perpendicular on the top edge of one F rectangle. Measure and mark a dot 3" to the left of the top right corner of G, then draw a diagonal line from the dot to the lower right corner of G. Sew on the drawn line; trim seam to ¼" (Figure 3a). Then, refer again to Sew & Flip Corners to add a corner triangle on the lower left corner of F using an H square to complete one left leaf unit (Figure 3b). Make nine.

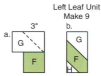

Left Leaf Unit
Make 9

Figure 3

4. Repeat step 3 to make nine right leaf units but position the G rectangle on the upper left of F and the H square on the lower right corner of F (Figure 4).

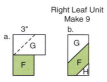

Right Leaf Unit
Make 9

Figure 4

5. Noting fabric orientation, arrange five different flower units, four D rectangles, two each E and I rectangles and one each left leaf unit, right leaf unit, and C, J and K rectangles in four rows. First sew the flower sections in the top row onto each side of the C rectangle, then sew a D rectangle on each side and the E rectangles on the top and bottom. Sew the remaining pieces into rows, then sew the rows together to complete one flower section (Figure 5). Make nine.

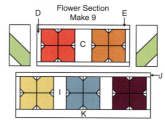

Flower Section
Make 9

Figure 5

6. Working with pieces in the same color family, sew one each L and M rectangle together lengthwise. Noting fabric orientation, refer again to Sew & Flip Corners to add a corner triangle on the lower left and lower right corners of L-M using two N squares to complete one L-M-N unit (Figure 6). Make nine.

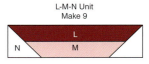

L-M-N Unit
Make 9

Figure 6

7. Position an I rectangle perpendicular on the left end of one O rectangle. Measure and mark a dot 2" down from the top left corner of I, then draw a diagonal line from the upper right corner of I to the dot. Sew on the drawn line; trim seam to ¼" (Figure 7a). Repeat on the opposite end of O using another I rectangle, but mark the dot 2" down from the top right corner of I, to complete one O-I unit (Figure 7b). Make nine.

O-I Unit
Make 9

Figure 7

8. Noting fabric orientation, sew one L-M-N unit on top of a matching O-I unit to complete one basket section (Figure 8). Make nine.

Basket Section
Make 9

Figure 8

9. Referring to the block diagram, sew a flower section on top of one basket section to complete one Basket block. Make nine.

Pinwheel

1. Refer to Half-Square Triangles on page 9 to make two T-U units using one each T and U square (Figure 9). Trim the units to 2" x 2". Make 160.

T-U Unit
Make 160

Figure 9

2. Noting fabric orientation, arrange four matching T-U units in two rows; sew into rows, then sew the rows together to complete one Pinwheel block (Figure 10). Make 40.

Pinwheel Block
Make 40

Figure 10

COMPLETING THE PINWHEEL BORDERS

1. Sew nine assorted Pinwheel blocks and 10 V squares alternating in a row to complete one side pinwheel border (Figure 11a). Make two.

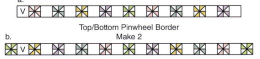

Side Pinwheel Border
Make 2

Top/Bottom Pinwheel Border
Make 2

Figure 11

Here's a Tip

Lay out the Pinwheel blocks on a design wall or large flat surface before sewing the borders to make sure colors are evenly distributed.

2. Sew 11 assorted Pinwheel blocks and ten V squares alternating in a row to complete one top/bottom pinwheel border (Figure 11b). Make two.

COMPLETING THE QUILT

1. Referring to the Assembly Diagram, arrange the Basket blocks, P rectangles and Q strips in five rows; sew into rows, then sew the rows together to complete the quilt center.

2. Sew the R border strips to the sides of the quilt center and the S border strips to the top and bottom.
3. Sew the side pinwheel borders to the sides and the top/bottom pinwheel borders to the top and bottom.
4. Sew the W–Z border strips onto the quilt in alphabetical order to complete the quilt top.
5. Layer, baste, quilt as desired and bind referring to Quilting Basics. The photographed quilt was quilted with an allover swirly design. ●

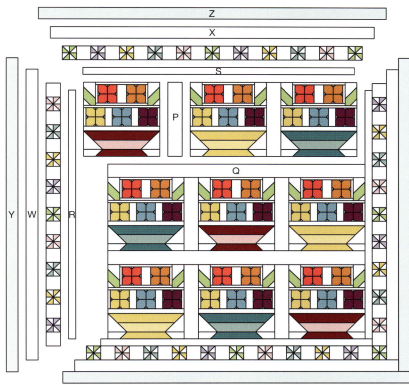

Blooming Baskets
Assembly Diagram 73" x 73"

DESIGN BY MATTHEW PRIDEMORE OF THE WHIMSICAL WORKSHOP
QUILTED BY CARRIE BOYLES

Sea of Color

A vibrant mix of colors in simple pieces make a complex whole.

SKILL LEVEL
Beginner

FINISHED SIZES
Quilt Size: 54" x 69"
Block Size: 15" x 15"
Number of Blocks: 12

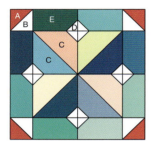

Block 1
15" x 15" Finished Block
Make 12

MATERIALS
- ⅔ yard coral #1 batik*
- 1 fat quarter each of coral #2, dark blue and light teal batiks* (3 total)
- 1 fat quarter each of 2 assorted blue, light blue, yellow, teal green, teal and dark teal batiks* (12 total)
- ⅞ yard coral #3 batik*
- 1 yard cream #1 batik*
- 2 yards cream #2 batik*
- 3½ yards backing*
- 62" x 77" batting
- Basic sewing tools and supplies

Fabrics from the Splish Splash collection by Heidi Pridemore for Island Batik used to make sample.

PROJECT NOTES
Read all instructions before beginning this project.

Stitch right sides together using a ¼" seam allowance unless otherwise specified.

Materials and cutting lists assume 40" of usable fabric width for yardage and 20" for fat quarters.

Arrows indicate directions to press seams.

WOF – width of fabric
HST – half-square triangle
QST – quarter-square triangle

CUTTING

From coral #1 batik cut:
- 6 (5⅞") C squares
- 6 (2" x WOF) F/G strips; stitch short ends to short ends, then subcut into:
  2 (2" x 60½") F and
  2 (2" x 48½") G border strips

From each coral #2, dark blue, blue #1 and #2, light blue #1, and yellow #1 and #2 batik fat quarters cut:
- 6 (5⅞") C squares (42 total)

From each light teal, teal green #1 and #2, dark teal #1 and #2, teal #1 and #2 and light blue #2 batik fat quarters cut:
- 12 (3" x 5½") E rectangles (96 total)

From coral #3 batik cut:
- 24 (3⅜") A squares
- 7 (2½" x WOF) binding strips

From cream #1 batik cut:
- 24 (3⅜") B squares
- 192 (2⅛") D squares

From cream #2 batik cut lengthwise:
- 2 (3½" x 63½") H border strips
- 2 (3½" x 54½") I border strips

COMPLETING THE BLOCKS

1. Referring to Half-Square Triangles on page 9, use A and B squares to make 48 HST units (Figure 1). If necessary, trim units to 3" square.

Make 48

Figure 1

2. In the same manner, use C squares to make 12 HST units in each of the following fabric combinations (Figure 2):
- Coral #1 / Blue #2
- Yellow #2 / Dark Blue
- Yellow #1 / Blue #1
- Coral #2 / Light Blue #1

Make 12   Make 12   Make 12   Make 12

Figure 2

3. Refer to Sew & Flip Corners on page 5 and sew D squares to opposite corners of the step 2 HST units as shown (Figure 3).

Make 12   Make 12   Make 12   Make 12

Figure 3

4. In the same manner, sew D squares to the lower right corner of the following E rectangles to make 12 of each unit as shown (Figure 4):
- Teal Green #1
- Teal #2
- Teal #1
- Light Blue #2

Make 12   Make 12   Make 12   Make 12

Figure 4

"The vibrant blues and teals of this collection led me to explore simple shapes that would create a complex feel when combined." —Matthew Pridemore

5. In the same manner, sew D squares to the lower left corner of the following E rectangles to make 12 of each unit as shown (Figure 5):
- Teal Green #2
- Dark Teal #1
- Dark Teal #2
- Light Teal

Figure 5

6. Refer to the Block 1 block diagram and arrange units in four rows as follows:
- Row 1: Step 1 HST unit, teal green #1 step 4 unit, teal green #2 step 5 unit, step 1 HST unit.
- Row 2: Dark teal #1 step 5 unit, coral #1 / blue #2 step 3 unit, yellow #2 / dark blue step 3 unit, teal #1 step 4 unit.
- Row 3: Teal #2 step 4 unit, yellow #1 / blue #1 step 3 unit, coral #2 / light blue #1 step 3 unit, light teal step 5 unit.
- Row 4: Step 1 HST unit, dark teal #2 step 5 unit, light blue #2 step 4 unit, step 1 HST unit.

7. Sew the units together in rows; join the rows to make 12 blocks.

COMPLETING THE QUILT

1. Refer to the Assembly Diagram and arrange the blocks in four rows of three blocks. Sew blocks together in rows; join the rows to make the quilt center.

2. Sew the border strips to the quilt center in alphabetical order to complete the quilt top.

3. Layer, baste, quilt as desired and bind referring to Quilting Basics. The photographed quilt was quilted with an edge-to-edge design of waves and fish. ●

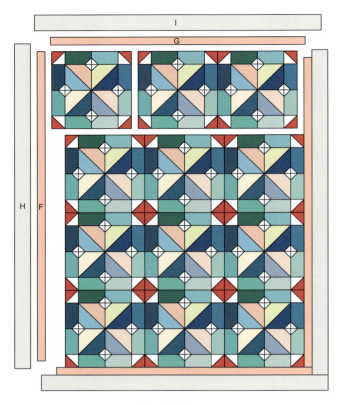

Sea of Color
Assembly Diagram 54" x 69"

Window Box

Quickly transform 10 fat quarters into a fun geometric throw quilt!

SKILL LEVEL
Confident Beginner

FINISHED SIZES
Quilt Size: 48" x 60"
Block Size: 12" x 12"
Number of Blocks: 20

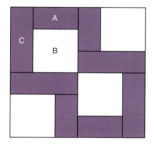

Window Box
12" x 12" Finished Block
Make 20

MATERIALS
- 10 assorted fat quarters*
- 1½ yards white solid*
- ½ yard orange tone-on-tone*
- 3⅓ yards backing
- 56" x 68" batting*
- Basic sewing tools and supplies

Fabrics from the Fossil Fern Basic and Superior Solids collections from Benartex; Tuscany Wool/Cotton Blend Batting by Hobbs Bonded Fibers used to make sample.

PROJECT NOTES
Read all instructions before beginning this project.

Stitch right sides together using a ¼" seam allowance unless otherwise specified.

Materials and cutting lists assume 40" of usable fabric width for yardage and 20" for fat quarters.

Arrows indicate directions to press seams.

WOF – width of fabric
HST – half-square triangle
QST – quarter-square triangle

Here's a Tip

This design would be great to feature nearly any fabric line, or 10 favorite fat quarters pulled from your stash!

CUTTING

From each fat quarter cut:
- 2 (2½" x 20") A strips
- 8 (2½" x 6½") C rectangles

From white solid cut:
- 20 (4½" x 20") B strips

From orange tone-on-tone cut:
- 6 (2½" x WOF) binding strips

COMPLETING THE BLOCKS
1. Join an assorted A strip and a white B strip to make a strip set (Figure 1). Make two with each fat quarter fabric. From each strip set, cut four A-B segments 4½" wide (eight per fat quarter fabric).

Make & cut 2 strip sets per fat quarter

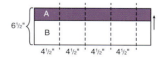

Figure 1

2. Sew a matching C rectangle to each A-B segment (Figure 2). Make 20 sets of four matching.

Make 4 per block

Figure 2

3. Arrange and sew two rows of two matching units each (Figure 3). Join the rows to complete the Window Box block. Make 20 total.

Make 20

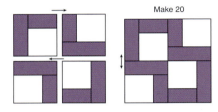

Figure 3

COMPLETING THE QUILT

1. Referring to the Assembly Diagram, lay out the blocks in five rows of four blocks each, noting the rotation of the blocks.

2. Sew the blocks into rows and join the rows to complete the quilt top. Press.

3. Layer, baste, quilt as desired and bind referring to Quilting Basics. The photographed quilt was quilted with an edge-to-edge diagonal serpentine design. ●

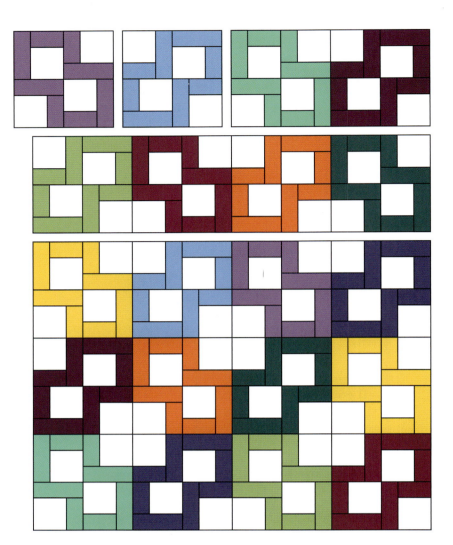

Window Box
Assembly Diagram 48" x 60"

"A gorgeous collection of Fossil Fern fat quarters from Benartex inspired this quilt. I knew I had to transform them into a quilt that would make the colors pop and shine!" —Rachelle Craig

DESIGNED & QUILTED BY PREETI HARRIS

Dreaming of Daylilies

Creatively pieced flowers highlight this colorful chain.

SKILL LEVEL
Confident Beginner

FINISHED SIZES
Quilt Size: 52" x 52"
Block Size: 16" x 16"
Number of Blocks: 9

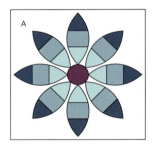

Daylily
16" x 16 Finished Block
Make 4

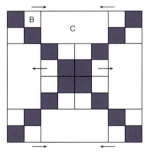

Irish Chain
16" x 16 Finished Block
Make 5

MATERIALS
- 17 assorted 2½" strips*
- 3⅓ yards background batik*
- 1¾ yards 20"-wide paper-backed fusible web
- Template material
- 3⅜ yards backing*
- 60" x 60" batting
- Basic sewing tools and supplies

Fabrics from the Poetic Bouquet collection by Island Batik used to make sample.

PROJECT NOTES
Read all instructions before beginning this project.

Stitch right sides together using a ¼" seam allowance unless otherwise specified.

Materials and cutting lists assume 40" of usable fabric width.

Arrows indicate directions to press seams.

WOF – width of fabric
HST – half-square triangle ◨
QST – quarter-square triangle ⊠

CUTTING

From assorted 2½" strips:
- Select four sets of light, medium and dark strips for Daylily blocks (12 total); from each strip cut:
  1 (2½" x 30") strip
- Set aside five strips for Irish Chain blocks

From background batik cut:
- 4 (16½") A squares
- 20 (4½" x 8½") C rectangles
- 5 (2½" x WOF) B strips
- 6 (2½" x WOF) D/E strips, stitch short ends to short ends, then subcut into:
  2 (2½" x 52½") E and
  2 (2½" x 48½") D border strips
- 6 (2½" x WOF) binding strips

From paper-backed fusible web cut:
- 4 (6¼" x 30") strips
- 4 (2½") squares

COMPLETING THE BLOCKS

Daylily

1. Sew one set of light, medium and dark 2½" x 30" strips together along the length with the medium strip in the middle (Figure 1). Press well; apply one 6¼" x 30" strip of paper-backed fusible web to the wrong side of the strip set following manufacturer's instructions. Make four.

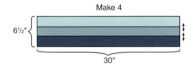

Make 4
6½"
30"

Figure 1

2. Prepare templates for melon and circle shapes from provided patterns.
3. Cut eight melon shapes from each step 1 strip set for a total of 32 (Figure 2).

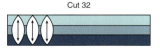

Cut 32

Figure 2

4. Referring to the quilt photo, cut four 2½" squares for the daylily centers. Apply 2½" square of paper-backed fusible web to the wrong side of each square and cut one circle shape from each.

5. Fold an A square in half vertically; press to crease. Repeat along horizontal and both diagonals. Make four.

6. Referring to Raw-Edge Fusible Appliqué on page 24, remove paper backing from one circle shape and one set of melon shapes; place them on one A square along the pressed lines with the light fabrics toward the center as shown in the Daylily block diagram, and press in place following manufacturer's instructions.

7. Machine-stitch shapes in place along the raw edge using a blanket stitch or a straight stitch ⅛" from the raw edge to complete the Daylily block. Make four.

Irish Chain

1. Stitch one reserved 2½"-wide strip to one B strip along the length (Figure 3). Make five strip sets. Cut 16 (2½"-wide) segments from each strip set for a total of 80.

Figure 3

2. Sew together two matching step 1 segments to make one four-patch unit (Figure 4). Make 40.

Figure 4

3. Refer to the Irish Chain block diagram and arrange eight matching four-patch units and four C rectangles into three rows. Sew the units and rectangles together in rows; join the rows to make one block. Make five.

COMPLETING THE QUILT

1. Refer to the Assembly Diagram and arrange the blocks as shown. Sew the blocks together in rows; join the rows to complete the quilt center.

2. Sew the border strips to the quilt center in alphabetical order to complete the quilt top.

3. Layer, baste, quilt as desired and bind referring to Quilting Basics. The photographed quilt was machine quilted in a grid using a serpentine stitch. ●

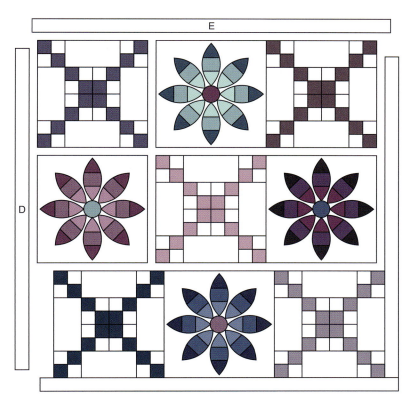

Dreaming of Daylilies
Assembly Diagram 52" x 52"

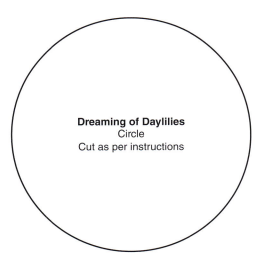

Dreaming of Daylilies
Circle
Cut as per instructions

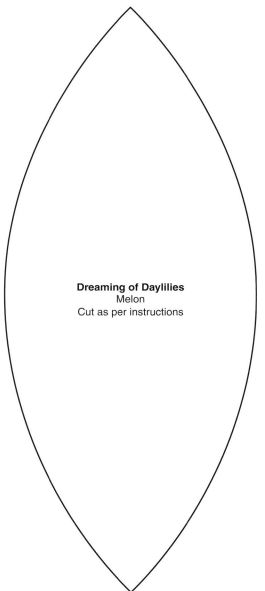

Dreaming of Daylilies
Melon
Cut as per instructions

RAW-EDGE FUSIBLE APPLIQUÉ

One of the easiest ways to appliqué is the raw-edge fusible-web method. Individual pieces of paper-backed fusible web are fused to the wrong side of specified fabrics, cut out and then fused together in a motif or individually to a foundation fabric, where they are machine-stitched in place.

Choosing Appliqué Fabrics

Depending on the appliqué, you may want to consider using batiks. Batik is a much tighter weave and, because of the manufacturing process, does not fray. If you are thinking about using regular quilting cottons, be sure to stitch your raw-edge appliqués with blanket/buttonhole stitches instead of a straight stitch.

Cutting Appliqué Pieces

1. Fusible appliqué shapes should be reversed for this technique.

2. Trace the appliqué shapes onto the paper side of paper-backed fusible web. Leave at least ¼" between shapes. Cut out shapes leaving a margin around traced lines. **Note:** *If doing several identical appliqués, trace reversed shapes onto template material to make reusable templates for tracing shapes onto the fusible web.*

3. Follow manufacturer's instructions and fuse shapes to wrong side of fabric as indicated on pattern for color and number to cut.

4. Cut out appliqué shapes on traced lines. Remove paper backing from shapes.

5. Again following fusible web manufacturer's instructions, arrange and fuse pieces to quilt referring to quilt pattern. Or fuse together shapes on top of an appliqué ironing mat to make an appliqué motif that can then be fused to the quilt.

Stitching Appliqué Edges

Machine-stitch appliqué edges to secure the appliqués in place and help finish the raw edges with matching or invisible thread (Photo A). **Note:** *To show stitching, all samples have been stitched with contrasting thread.*

Photo A

Invisible thread can be used to stitch appliqués down when using the blanket or straight stitches. Do not use it for the satin stitch. Definitely practice with invisible thread before using it on your quilt; it can sometimes be difficult to work with.

A short, narrow buttonhole or blanket stitch is most commonly used (Photo B). Your machine manual may also refer to this as an appliqué stitch. Be sure to stitch next to the appliqué edge with the stitch catching the appliqué.

Photo B

Photo C

Practice turning inside and outside corners on scrap fabric before stitching appliqué pieces. Learn how your machine stitches so that you can make the pivot points smooth (Photo C).

1. To stitch outer corners, stitch to the edge of the corner and stop with needle in the fabric at the corner point. Pivot to the next side of the corner and continue to sew (Photo D). You will get a box on an outside corner.

Photo D

2. To stitch inner corners, pivot at the inner point with needle in fabric (Photo E). You will see a Y shape in the corner.

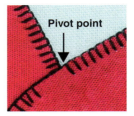
Photo E

3. You can also use a machine straight stitch. Turn corners in the same manner, stitching to the corners and pivoting with needle in down position (Photos F and G).

Photo F

Photo G

General Appliqué Tips

1. Use a light- to medium-weight stabilizer behind an appliqué to keep the fabric from puckering during machine stitching (Photo H).

Photo H

2. To reduce the stiffness of a finished appliqué, cut out the center of the fusible web shape, leaving ¼"–½" inside the pattern line. This gives a border of adhesive to fuse to the background and leaves the center soft and easy to quilt.

3. If an appliqué fabric is so light colored or thin that the background fabric shows through, fuse a lightweight interfacing to the wrong side of the fabric. You can also fuse a piece of the appliqué fabric to a matching piece, wrong sides together, and then apply the fusible web with a drawn pattern to one side. ●

DESIGN BY WENDY SHEPPARD
QUILTED BY DARLENE SZABO OF SEW GRACEFUL QUILTING

Lollipops

Precut bundles are such great ways to achieve a natural scrappy look!

SKILL LEVEL
Confident Beginner

FINISHED SIZES
Quilt Size: 49" x 58"
Block Size: 8" x 8"
Number of Blocks: 30

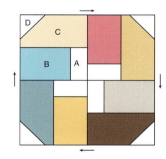

Lollipop
8" x 8" Finished Block
Make 30

MATERIALS
- 2⅛ yards white solid*
- 40 assorted 2½" strips*
- ⅝ yard coordinating print*
- 3¼ yards backing*
- 57" x 66" batting*
- Thread*
- Basic sewing tools and supplies

Fabrics from the Sunday Brunch collection by BasicGrey for Moda Fabrics; 50 wt. thread from Aurifil; Tuscany Silk batting from Hobbs Bonded Fibers used to make sample. EQ8 was used to design this quilt.

PROJECT NOTES
Read all instructions before beginning this project.

Stitch right sides together using a ¼" seam allowance unless otherwise specified.

Materials and cutting lists assume 40" of usable fabric width.

Arrows indicate directions to press seams.

WOF – width of fabric
HST – half-square triangle
QST – quarter-square triangle

CUTTING

From white solid cut:
- 120 (2") D squares
- 120 (1½" x 2½") A rectangles
- 49 (1½" x 8½") E strips
- 6 (3" x WOF) G/H strips, stitch short ends to short ends, then subcut into:
    2 (3" x 53½") G and
    2 (3" x 49½") H border strips

From 2 assorted 2½" strips cut:
- 20 (1½") F squares

From remaining assorted 2½" strips cut:

- 120 (2½" x 4½") C rectangles
- 120 (2½" x 3½") B rectangles

From coordinating print cut:

- 7 (2½" x WOF) binding strips

COMPLETING THE BLOCKS

1. Sew one A rectangle to one B rectangle (Figure 1). Make 120.

Make 120

Figure 1

2. Add one C rectangle to the top of one step 1 unit as shown (Figure 2). Make 120.

Make 120

Figure 2

3. Refer to Sew & Flip Corners on page 5 and sew a D square to the top left corner of each step 2 unit as shown (Figure 3).

Make 120

Figure 3

4. Refer to the Lollipop block diagram and arrange four step 3 units in two rows of two units as shown, rotating units as needed. Sew the units together in rows; join the rows to make one block. Make 30.

COMPLETING THE QUILT

1. Referring to the Assembly Diagram, sew together five blocks alternating with E strips to make a block row. Make six.

2. Sew together five E strips alternating with four matching F squares to make a sashing row. Make five.

3. Sew the block rows alternating with the sashing rows to make the quilt center.

4. Sew the border strips to the quilt center in alphabetical order to make the quilt top.

5. Layer, baste, quilt as desired and bind referring to Quilting Basics. The photographed quilt was quilted with a large floral design. ●

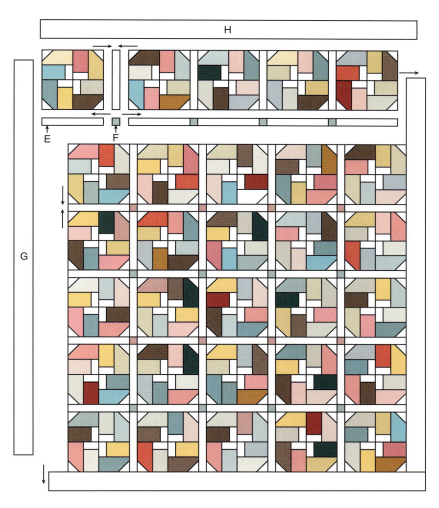

Lollipops
Assembly Diagram 49" x 58"

DESIGNED & QUILTED BY ANNETTE FALVO

Granny's Lemonade

The classic granny square gets a refreshing splash with some yellow and pink corner treatments.

SKILL LEVEL
Confident Beginner

FINISHED SIZES
Quilt Size: 53½" x 68"
Block Size: 12½" x 12½"
Number of Blocks: 12

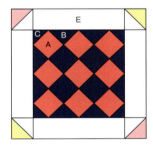

Granny's Lemonade
12½" x 12½" Finished Block
Make 12

MATERIALS
- 12 precut 2½" print strips*
- 1½ yards navy solid*
- 1⅝ yards white solid*
- ¼ yard yellow solid*
- ¼ yard pink solid*
- 1⅛ yards green solid*
- ⅝ yard purple solid*
- 4⅝ yards backing*
- 62" x 76" batting
- Basic sewing tools and supplies

Fabrics from the Kimberbell Basics and Kimberbell Solids collections by Maywood Studio used to make sample.

PROJECT NOTES
Read all instructions before beginning this project.

Stitch right sides together using a ¼" seam allowance unless otherwise specified.

Materials and cutting lists assume 40" of usable fabric width.

Arrows indicate directions to press seams.

WOF – width of fabric
HST – half-square triangle ◻
QST – quarter-square triangle ⊠

CUTTING

From each precut 2½" print strip cut:
- 9 (2½") A squares

From navy solid cut:
- 12 (4¼") B squares, then cut twice diagonally ⊠
- 24 (2⅜") C squares, then cut once diagonally ◻
- 68 (2½") A squares
- 7 (2½" x WOF) strips, stitch short ends to short ends, then subcut into:
  2 (2½" x 64½") G border strips and
  2 (2½" x 54") H border strips

From white solid cut:
- 10 (5¾") D squares
- 62 (2½" x 9") E rectangles

From yellow solid cut:
- 5 (5¾") D squares

From pink solid cut:
- 5 (5¾") D squares

From green solid cut:
- 31 (2½" x 13") F rectangles
- 18 (2½") A squares

From purple solid cut:
- 7 (2½" x WOF) binding strips

Here's a Tip

Lay out granny squares before adding white E rectangles and yellow and pink HSTs to make sure you have a color placement that is pleasing to your eye.

COMPLETING THE BLOCKS

1. Lay out nine matching print A squares, four navy A squares, eight navy B triangles, and four navy C triangles. Join into diagonal rows; join rows to complete a granny square (Figure 1). Make 12 granny squares.

Granny Square
Make 12

Figure 1

2. Referring to Eight-at-a-Time Half-Square Triangles, use white D squares and yellow D squares to make 40 yellow HSTs. Repeat to make 40 pink HSTs using white D squares and pink D squares (Figure 2).

HSTs
Make 40 each

Figure 2

3. Lay out one granny square, four white E rectangles, two yellow HSTs and two pink HSTs, noting color placement of the HSTs on opposite diagonals. Join as shown to complete a Granny's Lemonade block (Figure 3). Make 12 blocks.

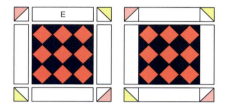

Granny's Lemonade Block
Make 12

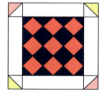

Figure 3

COMPLETING THE QUILT

1. Referring to the Assembly Diagram, lay out the blocks, navy A squares, green F rectangles, green A squares, white E rectangles and remaining HSTs into rows, noting the orientations of the blocks and placement of yellow and pink HSTs. Sew into rows; join rows together.

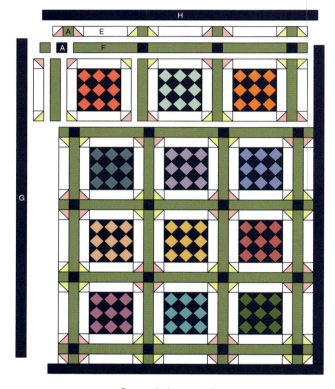

Granny's Lemonade
Assembly Diagram 53½" x 68"

2. Sew the G and H navy border strips to the quilt top in alphabetical order.

3. Layer, baste, quilt as desired and bind referring to Quilting Basics. The photographed quilt was quilted with a spiral design. ●

EIGHT-AT-A-TIME HALF-SQUARE TRIANGLES

Half-square triangles (HSTs) are a basic unit of quilting used in many blocks or on their own. This construction method will yield eight HST units.

1. Refer to the pattern for size to cut squares. The standard formula is to add 1" to the finished size of the square then multiply by 2. Cut two squares from different colors this size. For example, for a 3" finished HST unit, cut 8" squares (3" + 1" = 4"; 4" x 2 = 8").

2. Draw two diagonal lines from corner to corner on the wrong side of the lightest color square. Layer the squares right sides together. Stitch ¼" on either side of both drawn lines (Figure A).

Figure A

3. Cut the sewn squares in half horizontally and vertically, making four squares. Then cut each square apart on the drawn line, leaving a ¼" seam allowance and making eight HST units referring to Figure B. Trim each HST unit to the desired size (3½" in this example).

Figure B

4. Open the HST units and press seam allowances toward the darker fabric making eight HST units (Figure C). ●

Figure C

Sunset Strips

Log Cabin blocks create interesting waves in this fun design.

SKILL LEVEL
Confident Beginner

FINISHED SIZES
Quilt Size: 74" x 89"
Block Size: 14" x 14"
Number of Blocks: 20

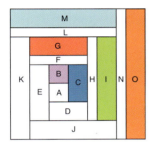

Log Cabin
14" x 14" Finished Block
Make 20

MATERIALS
- 4 yards white print*
- 40 (2½") assorted precut strips*
- 2¼ yards green print*
- 5½ yards backing*
- 82" x 97" batting*
- Basic sewing tools and supplies

Fabric from the Expressions Batiks Express Yourself! Ombre collection by Riley Blake Design; Warm & Natural: Warm 100 batting from The Warm Company used to make sample.

PROJECT NOTES
Read all instructions before beginning this project.

Stitch right sides together using a ¼" seam allowance unless otherwise specified.

Materials and cutting lists assume 40" of usable fabric width.

Arrows indicate directions to press seams.

WOF – width of fabric
HST – half-square triangle ◻
QST – quarter-square triangle ⊠

CUTTING

From white print cut:
- 20 (2½" x 11½") K rectangles
- 20 (2½" x 9½") J rectangles
- 20 (2½" x 6½") E rectangles
- 20 (2½" x 4½") D rectangles
- 20 (2½") A squares
- 4 (2" x WOF) strips, stitch short ends to short ends, then subcut into:
  2 (2" x 62½") Q strips
- 10 (2" x 14½") P rectangles
- 35 (1½" x 14½") N rectangles
- 20 (1½" x 11½") L rectangles
- 20 (1½" x 9½") H rectangles
- 20 (1½" x 6½") F rectangles
- 7 (1½" x WOF) strips, stitch short ends to short ends, then subcut into:
  4 (1½" x 62½") R strips

From assorted precut strips cut:
- 20 (2½" x 14½") O rectangles
- 20 (2½" x 11½") M rectangles
- 20 (2½" x 9½") I rectangles
- 20 (2½" x 6½") G rectangles
- 20 (2½" x 4½") C rectangles
- 20 (2½" x 2½") B squares

From green print cut:
- 8 (6½" x WOF) strips, stitch short ends to short ends, then subcut into:
  2 (6½" x 77½") S and 2 (6½" x 74½") T border strips
- 9 (2½" x WOF) binding strips

COMPLETING THE BLOCKS

1. Sew together one white F rectangle and one assorted G rectangle to make an F-G unit (Figure 1). Make 20. Repeat step 1 to make 20 H-I units, 20 L-M units and 20 N-O units.

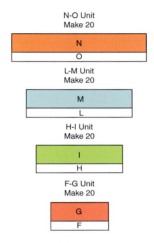

Figure 1

2. Lay out one white A square, one assorted B square, one assorted C rectangle, one white D rectangle, one white E rectangle, one F-G unit, one H-I unit, one white J rectangle, one white K rectangle, one L-M unit and one N-O unit as shown (Figure 2).

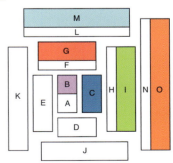

Figure 2

3. Sew patches and units together in alphabetical order to make a Log Cabin block. Trim to 14½" x 14½". Make 20.

Here's a Tip

A trick to sewing Log Cabin blocks is to turn the block a quarter turn counterclockwise after each seam so the seam that you just sewed is at the top and the strip you are adding goes on the right.

COMPLETING THE QUILT

1. Referring to the Assembly Diagram, lay out the blocks, white N rectangles, white P rectangles, white Q strips and white R strips as shown, noting the orientation of the blocks.
2. Sew into rows and join the rows to complete the quilt center. Press.
3. Sew the S and T border strips to the quilt top in alphabetical order.
4. Layer, baste, quilt as desired and bind referring to Quilting Basics. The photographed quilt was quilted with an overall hexagon design. ●

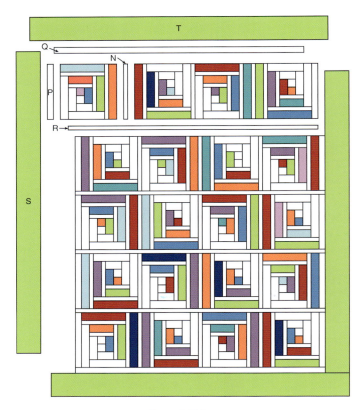

Sunset Strips
Assembly Diagram 74" x 89"

"Colorful butterflies returning to my garden each spring inspired this design." —Jen Daly

Jitterbug

A stack of 10" squares of your favorite fabric makes a flight of butterflies dancing amid a lattice of Irish Chain blocks.

SKILL LEVEL
Intermediate

FINISHED SIZES
Quilt Size: 71" x 71"
Block Size: 9" x 9"
Number of Blocks: 49

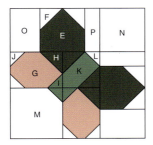

Butterfly
9" x 9" Finished Block
Make 25

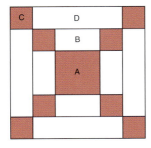

Irish Chain
9" x 9" Finished Block
Make 24

MATERIALS
- 39 precut (10") squares assorted prints*
- 3¾ yards cream solid*
- 1 yard border print*
- ¾ yard binding*
- 4½ yards backing*
- 79" x 79" batting
- Thread
- Basic sewing tools and supplies

*Fabrics from the Tango by Kate Spain and Bella Solids collections for Moda Fabrics used to make sample. EQ8 was used to design this quilt.

PROJECT NOTES
Read all instructions before beginning this project.

Stitch right sides together using a ¼" seam allowance unless otherwise specified.

Materials and cutting lists assume 40" of usable fabric width for yardage.

Arrows indicate directions to press seams.

WOF – width of fabric
HST – half-square triangle ◺
QST – quarter-square triangle ⊠

CUTTING

From each of 25 assorted print squares cut:

- 2 (3½") E squares (50 total)
- 2 (2¾" x 4¼") G rectangles (50 total)
- 1 (2¾") K square (25 total)
- 4 (2") H squares (100 total)
- 3 (1¼") I squares (75 total)

From each of 12 assorted print squares cut:

- 2 (3½") A squares (24 total)
- 16 (2") C squares (192 total)

From each of remaining 2 assorted print squares cut:

- 16 (2") R squares (32 total)

From cream solid cut:

- 25 (4¼") M squares
- 25 (3½") N squares
- 50 (2¾" x 3½") O rectangles
- 12 (2" x 9½") Q rectangles
- 112 (2" x 6½") D rectangles
- 96 (2" x 3½") B rectangles
- 104 (2") F squares
- 100 (1½") J squares
- 50 (1¼" x 3½") P rectangles
- 25 (1¼") L squares

From border print cut:

- 8 (3" x WOF) strips, stitch short ends to short ends, then subcut into:
  2 (3" x 71½") T and 2 (3" x 66½") S border strips

From binding cut:

- 8 (2½" x WOF) binding strips

COMPLETING THE BLOCKS

Irish Chain

1. Sew a B rectangle on two opposite sides of one A square to complete one A-B unit (Figure 1). Make 24.

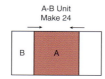

A-B Unit
Make 24

Figure 1

2. Sew a C square on the left end of one B rectangle, then sew a matching C square on the right end to complete one B-C unit (Figure 2). Make 48.

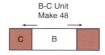

B-C Unit
Make 48

Figure 2

3. Sew a C square on the left end of one D rectangle, then sew a matching C square on the right end to complete one C-D unit (Figure 3). Make 48.

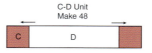

C-D Unit
Make 48

Figure 3

4. Working with matching pieces, sew a B-C unit to the top and bottom of one A-B unit, then sew a D rectangle to each side. Sew a C-D unit to the top and bottom to complete one Irish Chain block (Figure 4). Make 24.

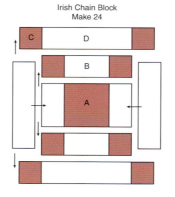

Irish Chain Block
Make 24

Figure 4

Butterfly

1. To make one Butterfly block, collect the following matching pieces: two E squares and four H squares. Also gather the following matching pieces: one K square and three I squares. Then choose two matching G rectangles.

2. Refer to Sew & Flip Corners on page 5 to add corner triangles on the upper left and upper right corners of one E square using two F squares to complete one E-F unit. (Figure 5). Make two.

E-F Unit
Make 2

Figure 5

3. Refer again to Sew & Flip Corners to add corner triangles on the upper left and lower left corners of one G rectangle using two J squares. Then add a corner triangle on the upper right corner using one H square. Add a corner triangle on the lower right corner using an I square to complete one left wing unit (Figure 6a).

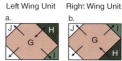

Left Wing Unit   Right Wing Unit
a.   b.

Figure 6

4. Repeat step 3 to make one right wing unit, but place H on the lower right corner of G and I on the upper right corner of G (Figure 6b).

5. Refer again to Sew & Flip Corners to add corner triangles on the upper left and lower right corners of the K square using the two remaining H squares. Then add a corner triangle on the upper right corner of K using an L square to complete one H-K-L unit (Figure 7).

H-K-L Unit

Figure 7

6. Refer again to Sew & Flip Corners to add a corner triangle on the upper right corner of one M square using the remaining I square to complete one I-M unit (Figure 8).

I-M Unit

Figure 8

7. Note fabric orientation in all remaining steps. Arrange the left wing unit, right wing unit, H-K-L unit and I-M unit in two rows; sew into rows, then sew the rows together (Figure 9a).

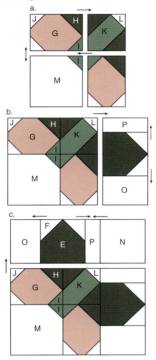

Figure 9

8. Sew a P rectangle to the top of one E-F unit, then sew an O rectangle to the bottom. Sew the step 7 unit to the left (Figure 9b).
9. Sew one O rectangle to the left of the remaining E-F unit and a P rectangle to the right. Sew one N square to the right of P, then sew the step 8 unit to the bottom to complete one Butterfly block (Figure 9c).
10. Repeat steps 1–9 to make 25 Butterfly blocks.

COMPLETING THE ROW END UNITS

1. Sew matching R squares to opposite ends of one D rectangle to complete one row end unit (Figure 10). Make 16.

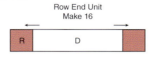

Figure 10

COMPLETING THE QUILT

1. Referring to the Assembly Diagram, arrange the Irish Chain blocks, Butterfly blocks, row end units, Q rectangles and remaining F squares in nine rows, alternating the blocks in each row. Sew into rows, then sew the rows together to complete the quilt center.
2. Sew the S border strips to the sides of the quilt center and the T border strips to the top and bottom to complete the quilt top.
3. Layer, baste, quilt as desired and bind referring to Quilting Basics. The photographed quilt was quilted with the Ginger Flight pantograph by Apricot Moon. ●

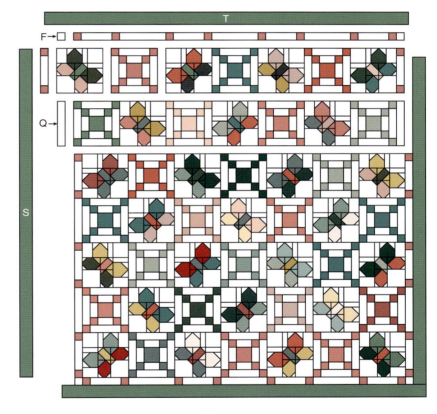

Jitterbug
Assembly Diagram 71" x 71"

Which Way Is Up?

This quilt is just the right size to piece and quilt on a weekend. All it takes is some fun fabrics and straight seam piecing.

SKILL LEVEL
Confident Beginner

FINISHED SIZES
Quilt Size: 52" x 64"
Block Size: 4" x 4"
Number of Blocks: 160

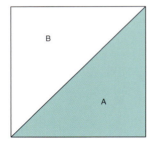

A-B
4" x 4" Finished Block
Make 160

MATERIALS
- 20–25 (10") squares*
- ⅝ yard red print*
- 2⅝ yards white solid*
- 3¼ yards backing fabric*
- 56" x 68" batting
- Thread
- Clearly Perfect Slotted Trimmer (optional)
- Basic sewing tools and supplies

Fabrics from the Blooming Colors collection by Wolff Paper for Benartex used to make sample.

Here's a Tip

Using a tool like a Clearly Perfect Slotted Trimmer makes trimming your HSTs easier.

PROJECT NOTES
Read all instructions before beginning this project.

Stitch right sides together using a ¼" seam allowance unless otherwise specified.

Arrows indicate directions to press seams.

Materials and cutting lists assume 40" of usable fabric width.

WOF – width of fabric
HST – half-square triangle
QST – quarter-square triangle

CUTTING

From 20–25 (10")
squares cut
- 80 (5") A squares

From red print cut:
- 6 (2½" x WOF) binding strips

From white solid cut:
- 80 (5") B squares
- 20 (4½") C squares
- 6 (2½" x WOF) strips, sew short ends to short ends, then subcut into:
  2 (2½" x 60½") D strips
  and 2 (2½" x 54½") E strips

COMPLETING THE BLOCKS
1. Referring to Half-Square Triangles on page 9, use A and B squares to make A-B blocks (Figure 1). Make 160. Trim to measure 4½" square.

A-B Block
Make 160

Figure 1

COMPLETING THE QUILT
1. Lay out the A-B Block and C squares into 15 rows of 12. Sew blocks and squares into rows and join the rows to complete the quilt center.
2. Sew D strips to opposite sides of the quilt center. Sew E strips to the top and bottom.
3. Layer, baste, quilt as desired and bind referring to Quilting Basics. The photographed quilt was quilted with a diagonal line design. ●

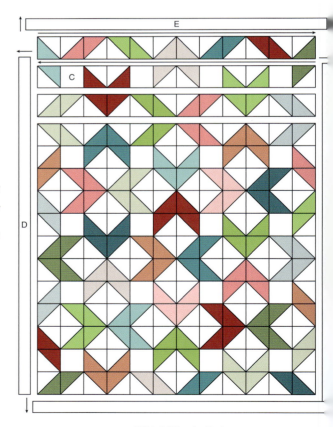

Which Way Is Up?
Assembly Diagram 52" x 64"

"I love using half-square triangles because they are so versatile, and this simple block can be arranged in endless ways to create a unique design. Use it alone or with another block, like I have here, to get the design you are happy with." —Mercedes Rose

Gentle Serenade

One Layer Cake® and some background fabric form a convenient and time-saving way to make a fun quilt.

SKILL LEVEL
Confident Beginner

FINISHED SIZES
Quilt Size: 60" x 72"
Block Size: 12" x 12"
Number of Blocks: 20

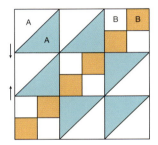

Gentle Serenade
12" x 12" Finished Block
Make 20

MATERIALS
- 30 assorted 10" x 10" squares*
- 2½ yards cream print*
- 1¼ yards light blue print*
- ¾ yard dark blue print*
- 4½ yards backing*
- 68" x 80" batting
- Basic sewing tools and supplies

Fabric from the Sunday Brunch collection by BasicGrey for Moda Fabrics used to make sample.

PROJECT NOTES
Read all instructions before beginning this project.
   Stitch right sides together using a ¼" seam allowance unless otherwise specified.

Materials and cutting lists assume 40" of usable fabric width.
   Arrows indicate directions to press seams.
WOF – width of fabric
HST – half-square triangle ◻
QST – quarter-square triangle ⊠

CUTTING

From each of 20 assorted 10" x 10" squares cut:
- 3 (5") A squares

From each of 10 assorted 10" x 10" squares cut:
- 3 (2½" x 10") B rectangles

From cream print cut:
- 60 (5") A squares
- 30 (2½" x 10¼") B rectangles
- 6 (2½" x WOF) strips, stitch short ends to short ends, then subcut into: 2 (2½" x 60½") C and 2 (2½" x 52½") D border strips

From light blue print cut:
- 7 (4½" x WOF) strips, stitch short ends to short ends, then subcut into: 2 (4½" x 64½") E and 2 (4½" x 60½") F border strips

From dark blue print cut:
- 8 (2½" x WOF) binding strips

COMPLETING THE BLOCKS

1. Refer to Half-Square Triangles on page 9 and use the cream A squares and assorted A squares to make 20 sets of six matching HST units (Figure 1).

HST Unit
Make 20 sets
of 6 matching

Figure 1

2. Sew together cream B rectangles and assorted B rectangles to make 10 sets of three matching strip sets (Figure 2). Cut each set of matching strips into 2½" segments to make 12 BB units.

B-B Unit
Cut 10 sets
of 3 matching
2½"

4½"

Figure 2

Here's a Tip

Center the assorted B rectangle on the cream B rectangle so there is extra fabric on each side of the assorted B rectangle. When you cut the segments, the last segment might be a little short of 2½", but the cream B rectangle will be the right size! When you sew the segments together you will still have an accurate 2½" unit to reference for your seam allowance.

3. Sew together two BB units as shown to make a four-patch unit (Figure 3). Repeat to make 10 sets of six matching four-patch units.

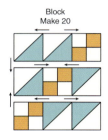

Four-Patch Unit
Make 10 sets of 6 matching

Figure 3

4. Lay out six matching HST units and three matching four-patch units into three rows. Join rows to complete a block (Figure 4). Make 20 blocks.

Block
Make 20

Figure 4

Here's a Tip

Try lining up the four-patch units so that they are all in the same color family in all of the diagonals that they form.

COMPLETING THE QUILT

1. Referring to the Assembly Diagram, lay out the blocks in five rows of four blocks each, noting the placement of the blocks.

2. Sew the blocks into rows and join the rows to complete the quilt center. Press.

3. Sew the C–F border strips to the quilt top in alphabetical order.

4. Layer, baste, quilt as desired and bind referring to Quilting Basics. The photographed quilt was quilted with a swirl design. ●

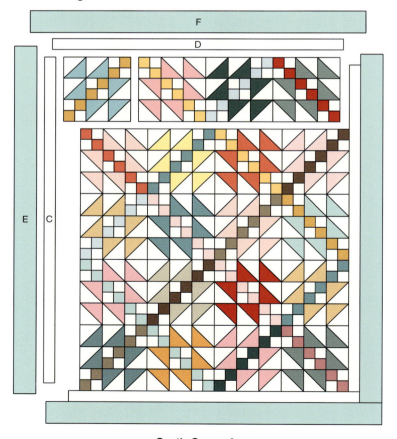

Gentle Serenade
Assembly Diagram 60" x 72"

Fleur de Vie

Lush, beautiful colors mingle together to create a stunning garden of blooming flowers that celebrate the joys of life and legacy.

SKILL LEVEL
Confident Beginner

FINISHED SIZES
Quilt Size: 61" x 61"
Block Size: 9" x 9"
Number of Blocks: 25

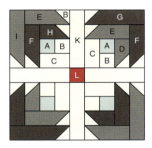

Block 1
9" x 9" Finished Block
Make 13

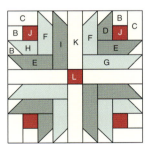

Block 2
9" x 9" Finished Block
Make 12

Here's a Tip

This quilt can also be made with 25 precut 10" squares, which will yield identical units in each block. of the diagonals that they form.

MATERIALS
- 50 sets of 2 matching precut 5" squares assorted prints
- 3 yards cream solid
- 1½ yards red tonal
- 1 yard light teal tonal
- 4 yards backing
- 69" x 69" batting
- Thread
- Basic sewing tools and supplies

PROJECT NOTES
Read all instructions before beginning this project.

Stitch right sides together using a ¼" seam allowance unless otherwise specified.

Materials and cutting lists assume 40" of usable fabric width for yardage.

Arrows indicate directions to press seams.

WOF – width of fabric
HST – half-square triangle ◻
QST – quarter-square triangle ⊠

CUTTING
Pair two coordinating sets of precut squares to make one block set of four squares, two squares each of two fabrics. Assemble 25 block sets.

Follow the cutting diagram to cut each square. Keep the cut pieces in each block set together.

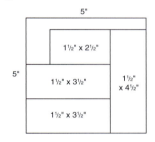

Cutting Diagram

From each block-set-fabric-1 square cut:
- 1 (1½" x 4½") I rectangle (2 total)
- 2 (1½" x 3½") E rectangles (4 total)
- 1 (1½" x 2½") D rectangle (2 total)

From each block-set-fabric-2 square cut:
- 1 (1½" x 4½") G rectangle (2 total)
- 2 (1½" x 3½") F rectangles (4 total)
- 1 (1½" x 2½") H rectangle (2 total)

From length of cream solid cut:
- 2 (1½" x 51½") O border strips
- 2 (1½" x 49½") N border strips
- 40 (1½" x 9½") M rectangles
- 100 (1½" x 4½") K rectangles
- 100 (1½" x 2½") C rectangles
- 500 (1½") B squares

From red tonal cut:

- 7 (2½" x WOF) strips, stitch short ends to short ends, then subcut into:
  2 (2½" x 61½") S and 2 (2½" x 57½") R border strips
- 7 (2½" x WOF) binding strips
- 48 (1½") J squares
- 41 (1½") L squares

From light teal tonal cut:

- 6 (3½" x WOF) strips, stitch short ends to short ends, then subcut into:
  2 (3½" x 57½") Q and 2 (3½" x 51½") P border strips
- 52 (1½") A squares

COMPLETING THE BLOCKS

Thirteen blocks are made with units that have A center squares. Twelve blocks are made with units that have J center squares. Determine which block sets will have A center square units and which block sets will have J center square units.

Block 1

1. Sew a B square to the top of one A square, then sew a C rectangle to the right to complete one A-B-C unit (Figure 1). Make 52.

A-B-C Unit
Make 52

Figure 1

2. Choose one block set of cut pieces that will have A center square units. Refer to Sew & Flip Corners on page 5 to add a corner triangle on the upper left corner of one D rectangle using a B square to complete one B-D unit (Figure 2a). Repeat to add a corner triangle on the lower right corner of one E rectangle using a B square to complete one B-E unit (Figure 2b). Noting fabric orientation, sew the B-D unit to the left of one A-B-C unit, then sew the B-E unit to the bottom (Figure 2c). Make two.

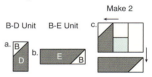

Make 2

B-D Unit   B-E Unit

a. b. c.

Figure 2

3. Refer again to Sew & Flip Corners to add a corner triangle on the upper left corner of one F rectangle using a B square to complete one B-F unit (Figure 3a). Repeat to add a corner triangle on the lower right corner of one G rectangle using a B square to complete one B-G unit (Figure 3b). Noting fabric orientation, sew the B-F unit to the left of one step 2 unit, then sew the B-G unit to the bottom to complete one unit 1 (Figure 3c). Make two.

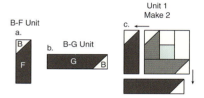

B-F Unit
a.

b.   B-G Unit

c.   Unit 1
Make 2

Figure 3

4. Refer again to Sew & Flip Corners to add a corner triangle on the lower left corner of one H rectangle using a B square to complete one B-H unit (Figure 4a). Repeat to add a corner triangle on the upper right corner of one F rectangle using a B square to complete one B-F unit (Figure 4b). Noting fabric orientation, sew the B-H unit to the bottom of one A-B-C unit, then sew the B-F unit to the right (Figure 4c). Make two.

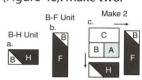

Make 2

B-F Unit
b.

B-H Unit
a.   c.

Figure 4

5. Refer again to Sew & Flip Corners to add a corner triangle on the lower left corner of one E rectangle using a B square to complete one B-E unit (Figure 5a). Repeat to add a corner triangle on the upper right corner of one I rectangle using a B square to complete one B-I unit (Figure 5b). Noting fabric orientation, sew the B-E unit to the bottom of one step 4 unit, then sew the B-I unit to the right to complete one unit 2 (Figure 5c). Make two.

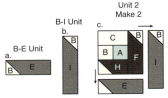

Figure 5

6. Noting fabric orientation, arrange the unit 1s, and unit 2s, four K rectangles and one L square in three rows; sew into rows, then sew the rows together to complete one Block 1 (Figure 6).

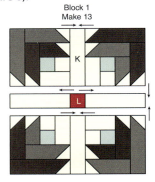

Figure 6

7. Repeat steps 2–6 to make 13 Block 1s.

Block 2

1. Sew a B square to the top of one J square, then sew a C rectangle to the right to complete one B-C-J unit (Figure 7). Make 48.

Figure 7

2. Repeat steps 2–6 in Block 1 to make 12 Block 2s using the remaining block sets of cut pieces and the B-C-J units instead of A-B-C units (Figure 8).

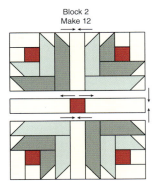

Figure 8

COMPLETING THE QUILT

1. Referring to the Assembly Diagram, arrange the Block 1s, Block 2s, M rectangles and remaining L squares in nine rows, alternating the blocks in each row. Sew into rows, then sew the rows together to complete the quilt center.

2. Sew the N–S border strips onto the quilt center in alphabetical order to complete the quilt top.

3. Layer, baste, quilt as desired and bind referring to Quilting Basics. The photographed quilt was quilted with an edge-to-edge design called Birds of a Feather by Christy Dillon. ●

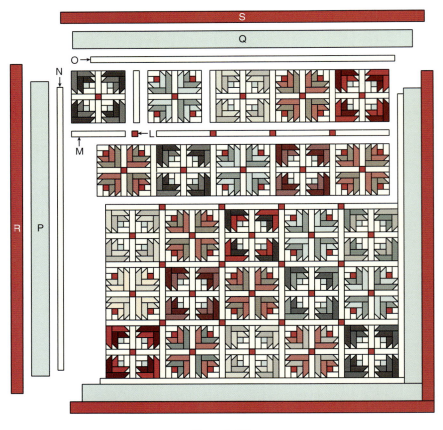

Fleur de Vie
Assembly Diagram 61" x 61"

Quilting Basics

The following is a reference guide. For more information, consult a comprehensive quilting book.

Quilt Backing & Batting

Cut your backing and batting 8" larger than the finished quilt-top size and 4" larger for quilts smaller than 50" square. **Note:** *Check with longarm quilter about their requirements, if applicable. For baby quilts not going to a longarm quilter 4"–6" overall may be sufficient.* If preparing the backing from standard-width fabrics, remove the selvages and sew two or three lengths together; press seams open. If using 108"-wide fabric, trim to size on the straight grain of the fabric. Prepare batting the same size as your backing.

Quilting

1. Press quilt top on both sides and trim all loose threads. **Note:** *If you are sending your quilt to a longarm quilter, contact them for specifics about preparing your quilt for quilting.*

2. Mark quilting design on quilt top. Make a quilt sandwich by layering the backing right side down, batting and quilt top centered right side up on flat surface and smooth out. Baste layers together using pins, thread basting or spray basting to hold. **Note:** *Tape or pin backing to surface to hold taut while layering and avoid puckers.*

3. Quilt as desired by hand or machine. Remove pins or basting as you quilt.

4. Trim batting and backing edges even with raw edges of quilt top.

Binding the Quilt

1. Join binding strips on short ends with diagonal seams to make one long strip; trim seams to ¼" and press seams open (Figure 1).

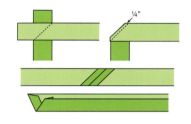

Figure 1

2. Fold ½" of one short end to wrong side and press. Fold the binding strip in half with wrong sides together along length, again referring to Figure 1; press.

3. Starting about 3" from the folded short end, sew binding to quilt top edges, matching raw edges and using a ¼" seam. Stop stitching ¼" from corner and backstitch (Figure 2).

Figure 2

4. Fold binding up at a 45-degree angle to seam and then down even with quilt edges, forming a pleat at corner (Figure 3).

Figure 3

5. Resume stitching from corner edge as shown in Figure 3, down quilt side, backstitching ¼" from next corner. Repeat, mitering all corners, stitching to within 3" of starting point.

6. Trim binding, leaving enough length to tuck inside starting end and complete stitching (Figure 4).

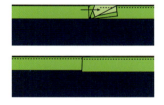

Figure 4

7. If stitching binding by hand, machine-sew binding to the front of the quilt and fold to the back before stitching. If stitching by machine, machine-sew binding to back of the quilt and fold to the front before stitching.

Special Thanks

Please join us in thanking the talented designers
whose work is featured in this collection.

Rachelle Craig
Carnival Confetti, 7
Window Box, 17

Jen Daly
Jitterbug, 35

Debi Estleman
Needlepoint, 2

Annette Falvo
Granny's Lemonade, 29

Scott A. Flanagan
Sunset Strips, 31

Preeti Harris
Dreaming of Daylilies, 20

Claudia Krider
Fleur de Vie, 43

Sue Pfau
Gentle Serenade, 40

Matthew Pridemore
Sea of Color, 14

Mercedes Rose
Which Way Is Up?, 38

Wendy Sheppard
Blooming Baskets, 10
Lollipops, 25

Supplies

We would like to thank the following manufacturers who provided
materials to our designers to make sample projects for this book.

Needlepoint, page 2: Fabrics from the Bee Dots and Bee Vintage Basics by Lori Holt and the Confetti Cotton collections for Riley Blake Designs; Heirloom Premium 80/20 batting from Hobbs Bonded Fibers.

Carnival Confetti, page 7: Fabrics from the 1895 Watercolors and 24/7 Solids collections from Hoffman Fabrics; Tuscany Wool/Cotton Blend Batting from Hobbs Bonded Fibers.

Blooming Baskets, page 10: Fabrics from Kimberbell Basics by Maywood Studio; 50 wt. thread from Aurifil; Tuscany Silk batting from Hobbs Bonded Fibers.

Sea of Color, page 14: Fabrics from the Splish Splash collection by Heidi Pridemore for Island Batik.

Window Box, page 17: Fabrics from the Fossil Fern basic and Superior Solids collections for Benartex Fabrics; Tuscany Wool/Cotton Blend batting by Hobbs Bonded Fibers.

Dreaming of Daylilies, page 20: Fabrics from the Poetic Bouquet collection by Island Batik.

Lollipops, page 25: Fabrics from the Sunday Brunch collection by BasicGrey for Moda Fabrics; 50 wt. thread from Aurifil; Tuscany Silk batting from Hobbs Bonded Fibers.

Granny's Lemonade, page 29: Fabrics from the Kimberbell Basics and Kimberbell Solids collections by Maywood Studio.

Sunset Strips, page 31: Fabrics from the Expressions Batiks Express Yourself! Ombre collection by Riley Blake Designs; Warm & Natural: Warm 100 batting from The Warm Company.

Jitterbug, page 35: Fabrics from the Tango by Kate Spain and Bella Solids collections for Moda Fabrics.

Which Way Is Up?, page 38: Fabrics from the Blooming Colors collection by Wolff Paper for Benartex.

Gentle Serenade, page 40: Fabrics from the Sunday Brunch collection by Basic Grey for Moda Fabrics.

Annie's®

Published by Annie's, 306 East Farr Road, Berne, IN 46711. Printed in USA. Copyright © 2025 Annie's. All rights reserved. This publication may not be reproduced in part or in whole without written permission from the publisher.
RETAIL STORES: If you would like to carry this publication or any other Annie's publications, visit AnniesWSL.com.
Every effort has been made to ensure that the instructions in this publication are complete and accurate. We cannot, however, take responsibility for human error, typographical mistakes or variations in individual work. Please visit AnniesCustomerService.com to check for pattern updates.

ISBN: 979-8-89253-385-0
1 2 3 4 5 6 7 8 9